TOMORROW MORNING, FAUSTUS!

□ TOMORROW MORNING, FAUSTUS! *An Infernal Comedy*

by *I. A. RICHARDS*

ROUTLEDGE & KEGAN PAUL London

First published in Great Britain in 1962
by Routledge & Kegan Paul Ltd.
Broadway House
68-74 Carter Lane
London, E.C.4
Printed in the United States of America
© I. A. Richards 1962

The categories in terms of which we group the events of the world around us are constructions or inventions. The class of prime numbers, animal species . . . squares and circles: all these are "inventions" and not "discoveries." They do not exist in the environment.

—*A Study of Thinking,* BRUNER, GOODNOW, and AUSTIN

TOMORROW MORNING, FAUSTUS!

DRAMATIS PERSONAE

SATAN: *elderly, tired, distinguished Personage;
Chairman of the Board*

BEELZEBUB: *harassed Executive; President*

MOLOCH: *vigorous brimstone General*

BELIAL: *elegant, dissolute Don*

MAMMON: *cultivated Financier*

SOPHIA: *Clerk of the Board, Wisdom Herself*

LORD FAUSTUS

PROLOGUE

Spoken by Marlowe's Faustus in Scarlet and Bonnet

I Marlowe's Faustus am, come back to tell
All here this truth: I never went to Hell.
All that was painted devils—bugaboo meant
To show me up as Hell-bound and Hell-bent.
Bent I was, true; could never "have grown full straight";
To be that serious was not my fate.
I was a grimly joke—I couldn't find
One jot of purpose in my tittling mind
So had to play with toys: with hopes and fears
You up-to-dates get through in preschool years.
This Doctor's rig—how should a Fool be dressed?—
It was the salt and pepper in the jest.
Fair Science, though, has learnt a thing or two;
To laugh at Doctorates today won't do.
Watch my successor now: he's off to Hell.
What happens there is for the play to tell.

Board Room of the Futurity Foundation, Inc. A large table with seats for five facing the audience. A separate table for the Clerk.

FIENDS *enter in any unexpected ways. For example, by suddenly stepping out from behind black screens placed behind their chairs.*

Enter MAMMON *and* MOLOCH.

MAMMON:
Morning Moloch!

MOLOCH:
                    Morning Mammon! It's
A good thing you and I, at least, have got
Some sense of time.

MAMMON:
                    And timing.

MOLOCH:
                    That's just it!
And timing. Haven't you noticed, Mammon?

MAMMON:
                    I certainly have!

MOLOCH:
Now that we've become a Foundation.

MAMMON:
                    Nobody cares.

MOLOCH:
Except you and me.

MAMMON:
Except you and I, Moloch.

MOLOCH:
                    Except you and me.

MAMMON:

Nobody except us ever arrives on time.

Enter BELIAL *and* BEELZEBUB. MAMMON *and* MOLOCH *pay no attention to them whatever.*

BEELZEBUB:

You know, Belial, I wouldn't wonder . . .

BELIAL:

I was just thinking the very same thing, Beelzebub.

BEELZEBUB:

I knew it, of course.

BELIAL:

Why not!

BEELZEBUB:

I'd rather say: "Why."

BELIAL:

You mean . . . ?

BEELZEBUB:

Yes, Why.

BELIAL:

There's a reason Why?
Don't you remember that good old song that went . . .

Sings slowly with viperish malice.

Take a goody good look
In the goody good book
There's a goody good reason Why!

BEELZEBUB:

I remember your writing it. Those were the good old days.

BELIAL:

The good old days before we were a Foundation.

BEELZEBUB:

Before we were a Foundation.

Enter SOPHIA.

BELIAL:
Good Morning, Sophy.

SOPHIA:
Good morning, Belial!

BEELZEBUB:
Do you know if Satan's had . . .

SOPHIA:
He's on his way.

MOLOCH:
I hope this time he isn't going to keep us waiting.

Enter SATAN.

SATAN:
All Present.
Then we may as well get started.

They all take their seats, SATAN *central in the Chair; on his right,* MAMMON *and* BELIAL; *on his left,* BEELZEBUB *and* MOLOCH; SOPHIA, *apart at her table facing them.*

SATAN (*putting on a lightly senile mood*):
Well, gentlemen, I need perhaps not take
A lot of time (although, no doubt, we've plenty)
Telling you what this meeting . . . er . . . is for:
A General Epochal Meeting, I observe.
The Clerk! Please note—although it's on this Notice
As all of you, of course, have seen. There has
Been some delay—not inappropriate,
I may perhaps remark: *epoche,* delay;
Epi, upon: *echo,* I hold. Right enough,
Don't you think, before an epoch ends
And a new age begins? (*Stretches and suppresses a yawn.*)
I rather wonder,
Sometimes, if we all of us realize
How serious these decisions of ours may be?
Yes, Belial?

BELIAL:
A slight point, Master: nowise a correction
But a clarification! Am I wrong

In thinking that an epoch is a *point*
To and from which a period is dated
And not itself a period at all—
Except, of course, as a full stop is one?

SATAN:

Very much to the point, Belial, I must say.

BELIAL:

And isn't it ἐπέχειν here rather than *echo?*

SATAN:

I'm sure you're right.

BELIAL:

It makes a difference.

SATAN:

I'm sure it must do. Won't you tell us how?

BELIAL:

This long delay there's been complaint about,
This holding back and putting off again,
This prudence some have called "procrastination,"
Others "irresolution," milder terms,
As we all know too well! "Sentiment,"
"Softheartedness," "Humanitarianism,"
Even "Loving-kindness" we have had to bear.
And why? Because we have waited, waiting on,
Watching for the exact point—the turning point—
To come

MOLOCH:

In my opinion, it's long past already.

BELIAL:

Ever the same sweet Moloch! rough and ready!

MOLOCH:

Ready, maybe. As a soldier, I can say
You never are, you cannot be, too ready.
But rough? I hope not. No. A decent margin
Within that, the pin point! Press hard where you choose!
Exact.

(*Demonstrates by dropping a paper clip like a bomb.*)

MAMMON:

Your two World Wars, for example, so precise,
So economical, so inexpensive!

SATAN:

Gentlemen! It might be easiest
If we became a little bit more formal.
May I call, formally, on our President,
And after him on the Vice Presidents in turn,
To present appreciations of our whole position?
And as your Chairman, Chairman of the Board,
—Mammon and Moloch will, I know, understand—
May I suggest questions and necessary comment
Be either postponed or addressed here to the Chair?
Beelzebub.

BEELZEBUB:

Glad indeed. Make a few remarks.
Afraid—after all this on pin points and precision—
Necessary vagueness.

MOLOCH:

Could you not ask him, sir, to speak more clearly?
I can't bear vagueness.

SATAN (*to* BEELZEBUB):

Moloch's a little
Hard of hearing; he can't hear you.

BEELZEBUB:

Of course!
Sorry Moloch! Well, as I was saying,
What little can be said, can't be said clearly.
It isn't clear itself, at most, not yet,
I rather doubt if ever it can be clear.
When it seems clear, so far, there's nothing in it
Or else we were not looking. We all know
Our Moloch's ancient taste for metaphysics
—*Ultra*physics now perhaps a better term—
Well, seeing *isn't* believing; seeing's finding
And we don't find, I trust, what isn't there!
So my report cannot be very lucid

Nor even brief, if brevity were our aim.

Some time ago, our Intelligence advising,
We placed, you will recall, a certain Faust . . .

BELIAL:

I have, I fear, a serious question for the Chair.

SATAN:

Yes, Belial, what is it?

BELIAL:

The President said FAUST. I call him FAUSTUS.
Is it the self-same man we are talking of?

Up front appears FAUSTUS *in his study sitting at a card table covered with papers. Behind him is a bare blackboard. He is about as far from* SOPHIA *as she is from the* FIENDS. *She turns to regard him. The* FIENDS *black out.*

FAUSTUS:

This interview's not easy. It's with some
Should know me well, but don't at all, I see:

FAUSTUS *scans imaginary faces of the* FIENDS *as if they were before him.*

Wide-eyed and smiling, else expressionless,
Companions not exactly eager to agree
Or in the mood to let me strike them dumb.

Shrugs his shoulders.

No good forecasting even in the round
What they will, or what I may, have to say;
Best leave all to the moment and the whim,
Trick out such ultimate business as a play
You improvise in, free to shift your ground.

Routine vapidities (leisurely warming up
For a snatch take-off) we'll trundle round.

With hand on table imitates plane taking station on runway.

No seat belt though, merely a cigarette.

Takes one.

Is it up to me to get us off the ground?
And what emotion's best as a stirrup cup?

Light on SOPHIA.

SOPHIA:
My serious Faustus thus prepares to die.
Worldly affairs wound up, his ignorant soul
Would plot her course by my inclining eye
Then most, when most, under her own control,
She seeks to be herself, as I am I:
A part reflecting, in herself, the Whole.

FAUSTUS (*addressing imaginary interlocutors*):
Contract? There was a Letter of Agreement.
I have my copy here—

Taking out letter.

                   not signed in fire,
Brimstone, or blood, nothing so bizarre.
To lay down firm the bounds of all desire
Black, lost-forever ink's my instrument.

Lays letter down and addresses imaginary FIENDS.

What breach on my part? None you dare allege
Offsets your total failure to conform!

Pauses and takes letter up.

Better reread in full, refer, recall,
Take bearings in this lull before the storm
Sound calmly now for reefs, feel out my edge.

Here is the bargain:

Reads (*and with repetitions*).

              "If they (or IT, through them)

Can tell, reveal, teach me, whatever way,
What I require to know (give me that power)
I'm to be theirs entire, my own SELF pay
As compensation full. . . . Any stratagem,

Device, contrivance, practice, ruse, disguise,
If used by either party for instruction,
—To teach or learn, explore, assay, try out:
That being the key objective of the action—
To be legitimate, not otherwise."

Very bad drafting! I forget now who
Put in which phrases; who hoped which clumsiness
Might give the taken-aback air room at need,
Who didn't care to note where carelessness
Could benefit the adversary too.

Benefit me perhaps. Or all of us?
They haven't taught, I haven't learnt a thing
Since that exalted hour when I called
And they responded: my conjecturing
Turned conjuring—three letters less of fuss!

Getting up and writing on blackboard. He is in high spirits.

CONJECTURING
CONJ   URING

E C T an ectomy indeed!
No appendectomy that! No knowing yet
What I lost or won by it. DISCOVERY
Gave place then to INVENTION. Don't forget
To what this make-believing was to lead.

They were to teach: I gave them ample powers;
I was to learn: I gave that all I had.
And nothing's happened. Everything's the same.
Inoperative the immitigable hours!
I know no more than then of good or bad.

As Faustus' study blacks out the lights go to SOPHIA *while she speaks and then take in the Board Meeting.*

SOPHIA:
When all have known—whatever else they could
Or could not know—have all at least known this,
Their trick of sorting out their bad from Good,

My sutler Faustus can't but take amiss
His fiends' incompetence, and well he should.
He's too near now. His homing echo off,
Distance receptors dead, he's in the trough.

As the Board Meeting returns, BELIAL *repeats his last speech.*

BELIAL:
The President said FAUST. I call him FAUSTUS.
Is it the self-same man we are talking of?

SATAN:
Beelzebub.

BEELZEBUB:
The same. And very much *not* the same, alas!
I am much indebted to my admired friend, Belial,
Who points his finger neatly to the switches
For all our mazy troubles. What's this FAUST
Or FAUSTUS? Settle that, all's clear.
I mean we then could shape a policy.
Till then, this Board itself, our corporate Will,
Must be at variance; our deepest grief,
The heart pang of our woe, taproot, and top,
Is our own lack of unity; and Man,
That bare chameleon, we don't yet know how,
Reflects our differences, might be an image
Thrown, flung, cast, molded on or in the void
Of us ourselves.

MOLOCH:
Impudent snake!
Better let me scotch it again and then
I won't say our little darling won't be maimed.

MAMMON:

   Mr. Chairman! Doubtless our brother Moloch
   Was addressing you. May I remark in turn
   We have ourselves to serve. These fluctuations,
   As Beelzebub sagaciously observed,
   Reflect—in ways not fully understood—
   Our own economy. Put it at the least:
   He is an Index, a useful Index of our state.
   Take up our Moloch's tender, his suggestion,
   Let him scotch Man again—not to say scorch—
   And where might we be then? If you would study
   My graphs (I have them in my Office, should you wish)
   You'll see enough to make even Moloch cautious.

BELIAL:

   If I . . .

SATAN:

   Yes, Belial?

BELIAL:

                 May take this further . . .
   I'd like to ask what really is our object?
   What do we hope to get through this Faustus after all?

MOLOCH (*interrupting*):

   I'd like to ask what Intelligence reports
   Of how our Faustus now is looking forward
   To our little talk tomorrow. (*Rubbing his hands.*)

BEELZEBUB:

                 Thank you, Belial.
   That takes us back to where we were before
   You raised your serious question. We use,
   I was saying, this Faustus as a *sound:*
   Not only as plummet or lead to attempt to fathom
   Or bring up samplings from what's called the bottom,
   To search out cavities, vacuities, and hollows.
   "To know your enemy," the old maxim goes,
   "Know where he is ignorant as well as knowing."
   Faustus is NOT our enemy, I need hardly say,
   If Moloch will permit me. We are told,

He is made in the image of his maker. But
Let us no rash extrapolations risk.
His knowledge should—if he's inspired—reveal;
But not his ignorances.

BELIAL:

                      If the Chair . . .
This image business has me a bit confused.
Beelzebub has made him out our image
Likewise his maker's, as he just now recalled.
For Mammon, he's that potent thing an Index,
Reflects our credit, almost is ourselves.
I rather wonder if this conjurer,
This changeling, this chameleon,
Who feeds on air, as the old stories have it,
This impresario, this illusionist,
Isn't acting up even on Mammon's graphs
To get himself more purchase. How much, I ask,
Is Faustus in on all this image stuff?

SATAN:

Not to add to these uncertainties,
These emptinesses swirling in this void,
I've sometimes taken Faustus as a blueprint
For some sort of new model of ourselves!

Spotlight on SOPHIA. FIENDS *black out.*

SOPHIA:

A part reflecting in herself the whole
Blueprint for a paradigm of conceiving:
In egg or work alike in-built the goal.

As she speaks she moves to stand behind Satan's chair.

These fiends of Faustus in their project weaving:
Fiend trivial (*pointing to* MAMMON)
         dull (*pointing to* BEELZEBUB)
   fantastical (*pointing to* BELIAL)
      or fell (*pointing to* MOLOCH)
Entangled in a cause past their retrieving,

Returns to her own table; FIENDS *are lit again.*

To wreck a universe re-create a soul.

MAMMON:

May I suggest we go on with the Report!

BEELZEBUB:

Willingly! Mindful of much of this
Here so far mentioned, we wrote this Faustus
A Letter of Agreement. Here it is.
I doubt not all your memories retain
Exactly its provisions. The main intent
Was to explore precisely how his lights—
Reflections, as we've said, of a light elsewhere—
Would apprehend and analyze its terms.

BELIAL:

You mean that Letter is our crystal ball
Our prism to sort out, split him like a spectrum;
Pry out, pry into all his modes of being. . . .

BEELZEBUB:

And ours as well, maybe? But let's remember
This isn't optics. It's biology.
It's Faustus' selves we are interested in viewing.
His styles of make-up, you might say, make-believe.
To gather these we had to implant a germ,
Having prepared a culture. We fed it well
And watchfully, and have developed thus
A speculum, so term it, which can yield
Whatever sample insights you may wish
Me to exhibit.

MAMMON:

                    "Fed it well," you say
May we hear more about this nourishment,
This pabulum for insight? Maybe we,
Ourselves—forgive me, Belial—
Might be the better for a dose of that?

Light on SOPHIA *only. As she speaks, her lines appear on the large white Screen that hangs over the Board Room table like a sound reflector. The* FIENDS *freeze into immobility as light leaves them.*

SOPHIA AND SCREEN:

What's said through me through me becomes devote:
Given and given up, its end attained,
Not to be played with more. My words denote
The limits of your license to amend.
What else is yours. Know that mind cannot think
Beyond. Its offering it must still subtend
For all its accurate stepping at the brink.

The Screen goes blank. Light and animation return to the FIENDS.

SATAN:

If you should so desire, we can have shown
Upon the Impending Screen for all to gaze at
The substance of that course, the nutriment,
With the digestive processes employed,
The assimilations, and the excrement.
Recall the advice I gave Man: "Know thyself!"
That rare advice I gave the fool at Delphi,
"Man, know thyself!"—much good may it have done him!
It was to know all this, inseparably, entire;
But privately: knower secluded with his knowledge.
What's on that Screen is monitored in heaven.
We have some secrets still, at least, you trust so.

BELIAL:

Foul souls have called *us* heaven's excrement.

MOLOCH:

One of them, I think, had Belial in mind.

SATAN:

My followers, companions, friends of old
And fellows then—these late divisions,
These strains within our body, reappear
Perforce within this Instrument of ours.
If we project the history of Faustus,
His genesis and nurture, on that Screen

All this within ourselves is there declared
And more, a record of it all's preserved.
I care not, much, for Man: tell *all* to Man
(To the most of men) tell nothing; although some few
Strangely *divine*—the Clerk will underline
That word—strangely *divine* (spies that they are)
The whole truth in a tittle. No, it's not Man
We have to beware of but the Adversary.
Our great traducer, Milton—that disguise
The author of our being then put on—
Hid from us this: whatever's on that Screen
Once shown, lapses from show, is "in the Record."

BELIAL:

Are you suggesting, sir, we re-enact
Here, for our own sake, ourselves the audience,
That old, well-studied parable of the Tree?

SATAN:

Re-enact it and re-edit; change the ending.

BELIAL:

Keep in our stations and obey the rules?
Let all the tempting tushery go hang?

Pointing up to the Impending Screen.

I, Belial, become a shrewder Eve!

SATAN:

Exactly. There are those who know themselves
Too well to know what's what. Are you perhaps so?

BELIAL:

I have no answer. I find the question curious.

SATAN:

It will be answered for you. Now, who is it
Would recommend that the Impending Screen should tell?

The FIENDS *look at one another in silence.*

BEELZEBUB:

To quiet these qualms, old hungers that will echo,
Let us return to Faustus. Bear in mind

That every view's a view, never the what
We would like to see, but a reverted vision.
To answer Moloch's earlier question, see
Here on our underviewer, here he is,
Our Faustus in his latest meditation
Deep sunk in his reflections

SATAN:

This completes
My right hand, here, Beelzebub's report.

Lights spread to FAUSTUS *at his card table as before, and* FIENDS *turn to watch him.*

FAUSTUS:

Suppose I know that THEY are listening in,
Observe my thought, as well as note my words.
It's likelier than not—so be they BE,
Aren't merely my own fancy's lively birds.
Plainly, if so, I don't have to begin!

Gets up and comes forward.

I've been on tap (*twists imaginary faucet*), I take it, all my
        life,
"Ever in my great Taskmaster's eye"
Taskmasters, in the plural, though, with me
And I suspect, with Milton too, or why
All that ambition, arrogance, and strife.

"By that sin fell the angels" wrote a greater—
And did not lose it through their fall, alack!
(Modesty would now the more become them)
Who take through me their route to clamber back
By the crack that splits the creature from creator.

Suppose I am some shadowings somehow thrown
Upon this rockhouse barrier, my mind.
(Let be, awhile, the film—whatever throws them—
Let be the light—or lights maybe—behind
Let doubt all doubts of how the show is shown)

With shadows, radiant clearings of lit ground,
Bright as salt, so lit, and pure as snow,
Through which the very grain of the wall can show.
What glint! What crumble! A bit dazzling though—
As the parent cave—in the eyeball here—has found.

You too, old fiends, what are you? What not? Who?
Patches of bright and somber? Not at all!
Initial signs at most initials are,
As ultimate as that the Earth's a ball!
To switch the image, are you planets too?

Half night, half day, a-sway in a seeming void
Stable because a-spin and swinging round,
Lost, desperate, frantic in your tethered flight
About your source, your dance deployed
To bring you ever whither you are bound.

Mocking imaginary FIENDS.

And do you shine in your own right as well?
Give back what you are given, in some measure,
But further, add? Conserve the sum of good,
Enhance it too? Reinvest your treasure?
Fine questions these . . . should tease these Lords of Hell!

Well, come what may, keep up the talk on goals.
And I should win my own share of the fun!
Those fellows think they have it in a hitch.
The question's: Which? and I've another one:
"All things that move between the quiet poles."

FAUSTUS *blacks out. Lights on* FIENDS *as before.*

MAMMON:
Well, Mr. Chairman, if I may say so, this
Is hardly the Report our President
Had led us to expect.

BELIAL:
                    Perhaps it is.
Not all were optimistic. Didn't Moloch
Raise his unheeded question at the start?
Beelzebub's reply then seemed evasive.
Now, it's plain ominous.

MOLOCH:
                    In any case,
None can deny now! It's gone past whitewashing!
This instrument, this sound, this speculum,
This crafty, expensive, O so secret product
Of slow contrivance, this high masterpiece
Of managerial art's no good at all.
The upstart worm presumes to mock at us.
Have I the Board's good leave to pash him?

MAMMON:
                    No!
We yet have uses for him. Mr. Chairman,
Recalling your and Beelzebub's strong pleas
For unity among us, I propose
—As our surest means of healing any breaches—
Wider participation. Moloch, Belial, and I
In this Faustus thing have been mere onlookers
And hardly that: the claims of secrecy
Shut us out uninformed. We've no idea
Of what you have or haven't done to him.
We do agree security forbids
Use of the Impending Screen, though Faustus seems
To have no strings on what he prattles of.
It's clear, though, he's deranged.

BELIAL:
                    Beyond a doubt!
I hazard the guess that he has been ill used
Too much, too long.

MOLOCH:
                    Piffle! We've not begun!

MAMMON:

    Anyway, it's plain he's out of order.
    But since—however, as yet, all's gone astray—
    The original plan, agreed on at the start
    By all of us in Council at our last . . .

BEELZEBUB:

                    The last but one.

MAMMON:

    Quite right! The General Epochal Meeting
    Before the one preceding this—agreed by all
    This Faustus should be prepared and lowered
    As grating, grid or psycho-spectrograph,
    Or what you will, to show what radiations
    From that suspected SOURCE (or sources) now
    We need watch out for most, then let us still
    Go on with him—but with this revision:
    That we three, Moloch, Belial, and I
    Now put him through our individual tests.

MOLOCH:

    I know what test I'd give him!

BELIAL:

                  So do I!

MAMMON:

    Tests circumscribed, devised, and calculated
    To bring out one or other character,
    Translucence or opacity in his Being.
    So, thereafter . . .

BELIAL:

                 We may the better savor
    The use that he can be to us in the project,
    Or, that failing . . .

MOLOCH:

               Wipe him off the earth.

BEELZEBUB:

    A point of order.

SATAN:

Yes, Beelzebub?

BEELZEBUB:

Perhaps a bit pedantic, but hadn't we better
Ask the Clerk to look up the paragraphs in our Charter
Authorizing us to devise and apply such tests?

SOPHIA:

They have already been looked up. It is in order.

SATAN:

Then it's all clear, I take it, President?

BEELZEBUB:

All clear. And may I profit by this chance
To say how happy we are to have such supplements
To our, no doubt, not too well guided efforts
Toward our common aim. I assume that you,
Lord Mammon, will begin the round. Your steps,
No question of it, will greatly extend our knowledge.

MAMMON:

I'll just send down a vehicle of mine
Through which I'll try him out. And—O yes—may I
Have the usual one-way presence on in force?

BEELZEBUB:

Standard exposures: feelings, thoughts, desires,
The lot. You know of course that this direct inspection
Of human minds can only operate
While we ourselves remain invisible
Or use an *undetected* vehicle.
The interference otherwise is too great.
However, among fiends . . .
And may I remind you—I feel like a stewardess
In one of those planes they are so proud to fly in—
Don't leave your private opinions in the open.
While this clairvoyancy Psy-ray field's in action
Whatever any of us may think, our personal feelings
Are more or less on show to all. We've had,

You will remember, one or two incidents,
Embarrassments, indiscretions, awkwardnesses,
I'm sure, we will all prefer to have no more.

BELIAL:
Hadn't we perhaps better . . .

BEELZEBUB:
Why yes, of course,
Belial reminds me we can take care of this.
As a precaution, no doubt unnecessary,
Here, for each of us we can now provide
New insulators . . .

Subordinate DEMONS *bring Headpieces to* BELIAL *and* BEELZE-
BUB *who hand them to others and help them to put them on.*

BELIAL:
You slip them on like this.
Now do you notice—I've switched the Psy-rays on—
A mild quietus, lessening of tension . . . ?
Try them off and on, aren't they restful?

MAMMON:
Most remarkable!

MOLOCH:
Rockaby, Baby!

SATAN:
Highly convenient!

BEELZEBUB:
These new screens, of course,
We owe in chief to Belial's special studies.

BELIAL:
For myself I've found them useful. Especially
In observations of the onset of seduction
And analogous enquiries. A later model
Will, I hope, be invisible, undetectable.
Handy when you are feeling charitable
Or merely diplomatic.

BEELZEBUB (*taking mask off*):
These covers off
We are open to each other. As to Faustus,

We'll see and hear him totally: thought and feelings.
He'll have your visitant, for the rest must guess.

BELIAL:

It's playing somewhat safe. Although I know him
I'd say he hasn't the frailest ghost of a chance.

MOLOCH:

Why we must play any game here's quite beyond me.
Why not make certain quickly while there's time?
What's power for? Use it while you have it.
But, if you *will* make it a gamble, mine's on him.

FAUSTUS *as before in his study. Owl hoots.*

FAUSTUS:

Ha! Hark at that! (*Owl hoots twice again fearsomely.*)
              If I were now my namesake,
Old Doctor Faustus back in Wertenberg,
I'd build a bit on that! (*Gets up and walks about.*)
              The random creaking
Of these old crazy boards, that crazy bird
(*Owl hoots again.*)
My crazy self that won't take note of omens
Well-omened Faustus won't! (*Owl hoots again.*)

"It was the owl that shriek'd, the fatal bellman
Which gives the stern'st good night."
"They say the owl was a baker's daughter.
Lord, we know what we are, but know not what
We may be!" Dear old Shakespeare! "Any stratagem,
Device, contrivance, practice, ruse, *disguise*"
Disguise . . . No use asking too hard of anyone, "Who are
      you?"
Ask yourself, and what do you get as an answer?
Best take things at face value while you can.

He takes a chair and places it as for a visitor.
Stands looking at the door. A soft knock.
FAUSTUS *nods and holds up a finger. Knock repeated.*

Come in!

Enter good-looking girl, career type, in a very good suit.

MAMMON VEHICLE:

You will forgive me, I hope, Lord Faustus. I've been sent
By the World Population Control Bureau, you know,
To ascertain your views on rationing.

FAUSTUS:

Rationing?

M-V:

Yes, how to allocate their quotas to the nations.

FAUSTUS:

My views! I haven't any. Leave me out.

M-V:

No views! How careless! As great a man as you
Has his responsibilities to the planet.

FAUSTUS:

Responsibilities! A girl like you
Has hers. What's your present line now? How many?

M-V:

I'm not quite sure, Lord Faustus, I understand you.

FAUSTUS:

How many babes will *you* have, that's my question.

M-V:

That, Lord Faustus, is entirely my own concern.
What children I have and when and whose and how
And the rest of it are a private personal matter.

FAUSTUS:

With which Population Control has nothing at all to do?
I doubt it. But, if so, so are my views.

M-V:

I hope, sir, you'll see that that's untenable.
You are a man of the highest possible intelligence.

FAUSTUS:

And what do you think you are?

M-V:

                Still, for all that . . .

FAUSTUS:

You want a story from me on population?

M-V:

The genetics angle with stress on the shortages.

FAUSTUS:

There are other angles. Remember your children may
Have the novel duty of voting for your demise.

The lights switch up to the Watchers.

BELIAL:

Your vehicle, Mammon, though I say it, is pretty smart!

MAMMON:

Thank you, Belial! From you! You ought to know!

BELIAL:

Better watch out, though! Don't forget our aim!
Don't let your succedaneum succumb!

MAMMON:

Ha! Green-eyed are we still, my Belial!

BELIAL:

No! But such tactics can be rather dazzling.

SATAN:

The aim is samplings of the suspect light.

Back to Faustus' study.

FAUSTUS:

Look here! Do you want quantity or quality?

M-V (*writing in her pad*):

"Quantity or quality?"

FAUSTUS:

The question is if you can have them both.

M-V:

"both"

FAUSTUS:

You want them both, of course, if you can get them.

M-V:

And can't you?

FAUSTUS:

Well, but can you? Tell me how.

M-V:

I should have thought modern technology,
Automation, novel sources of energy,
Improved training of operatives,
Shorter hours, higher efficiency,
Fuller use of leisure . . .

FAUSTUS:

And so on

M-V:

And so on

FAUSTUS:

and on and on and on . . .

M-V:

Yes

FAUSTUS:

Would?

M-V:

Yes

FAUSTUS:

Would?

M-V:

Why give us what we want: all of the best.

FAUSTUS:

You mentioned, or didn't you mention, education?

M-V:

Training of operatives, fuller use of leisure . . .

FAUSTUS:

And is that quite the same?

M-V:

I don't quite get you.

FAUSTUS:

It is not what's offered, or what's in supply,
But what they'll take that matters. That's the curve

To watch. That's the root of econometrics.
Too much may be more deadly than too little.

M-V:

A moral truth indeed! O sir, I'm dazzled!

FAUSTUS:

You might be if you followed it a bit further.
Take yourself now. You've looked into a mirror?
Don't look self-conscious! You have seen your nose.
You know, better than I do, why it's handsome.
Not too much or too little. You've generalized.
You've enough other examples lying handy.
You'd hope to be as just in thought and deed?
Or don't you?

M-V:

I'm here to take your message.

FAUSTUS:

Not here to think? I think you are better than that.

M-V:

I'm not here to talk of me, but for your message.

FAUSTUS:

O simply measure: the law of every craft
The life of the cell.

M-V:

      Very inter-esting!
But what has this to do with population?

FAUSTUS:

You don't work that out?

M-V:

You spell it out!

FAUSTUS:

You are up to something. What is it now? Confess!

The lights switch up to the Watchers.

BEELZEBUB:

I thought our man was being a little simple!
He wasn't. He'd begun to smell a rat!

MAMMON:

I must say how I relish your choice of phrasing.

BEELZEBUB:

Never mind that. I know it isn't easy
Being two or more people at once, I mean.
All the same, I'm warning you now: Look out!

MOLOCH:

Another damned professor! I don't trust him!
Goody-goody! It's he who'd better look out.

Back to Faustus' study.

FAUSTUS:

Don't be afraid! I'm not trying now to convert you.
He'd be an owl who thought anyone could do that!
No "Come to the Mercy Bench!" about all this!
Straight physiology: the balanced diet.

M-V:

I did hope you'd touch on the genetics.

FAUSTUS:

This is it and I'm wondering why you won't see it.

M-V:

Explain it if you can. I wonder if you can.

FAUSTUS (*as if to himself*):

A test! A challenge!
(*Soliloquy up front*) There's no test ever set
But tests the test along with what it's testing.
True too of the gene set and its setting.
As plants compete for light, food, water,
So peoples struggle for power; within that squeeze
The modes of power develop and what was power
Gives place to what will next be.
                                    It's not numbers
Even now that lift a nation; it's not money
(I see you smile); it's not mere energy.
What gives it *rank* is something else again.

M-V:

But what's this *rank?* You've changed your ground again!

FAUSTUS:

    I've not. I have to turn you in your socket.
    I have to use on you another idea.
    You are only feeling the other tongue of the pliers.

M-V:

    Rank isn't at all the same sort of thing as power.

FAUSTUS:

    You challenged me to explain, but will you let me?
    If I were to convince you, would you change your mind?

M-V:

    I don't like rank or brass. They don't play fair.

FAUSTUS:

    That isn't the game we are in, the game you are playing.
    The rank I tell you of is the new form of power.

M-V:

    I was told you were good at explaining. Never mind!

FAUSTUS:

    I do what I can, but there's always the explainee.

M-V:

    All right. Give me up as hopeless? Is that it?

FAUSTUS:

    Look. Power to destroy, as you know, destroys itself
    When it grows too great. That brings in a new power.
    It is that I am calling rank: courage to face
    The oncoming and do what has to be done.
    Two oncomings: one is the Third World War;
    The other the population pressure.
    Nations that can reconstruct themselves,
    Remodel how they will see it all soon enough,
    It is they who deserve a future. They may not get it.

M-V:

    Unilateral disarmament! Licenses
    For childbirth! How old-hat!

FAUSTUS:

                   You are in the fashion.
    And you know how fashions change.

M-V:
>Your new brand of power
Is a power just to fold up and lie down.
And you call that courage!

FAUSTUS:
>Don't overlook
How hard it must be to do it. Otherwise
There would be more movement on the narrow way.

M-V:
It's against human nature.

FAUSTUS:
>Maybe so,
Against the received models. But it has happened
All through our past that we who were to survive
Climbed up from the water, dropped down from the tree,
Did somehow the very thing that the others couldn't.
It has happened. It's still happening. Look around.
Quantity, I said, or quality. Quantity:
Echo-output of what's past. Quality:
The would-be instauration of a future.

M-V:
I didn't expect to find you so Idealist.

FAUSTUS:
Idealist yourself! You are spoiling for a row.

M-V:
A row with you! I know to whom I'm speaking.

FAUSTUS:
Do you indeed? What's making you so tense?
You are almost breaking the arms off. Spare my chair!

M-V (*standing up*):
I don't know why you are being so cross with me.

FAUSTUS:
I don't *know* either. I'm beginning to think I guess.

M-V:
I said Idealist. Should I have said, "Unworldly"?

FAUSTUS:

Which World might you be having in mind?

M-V:

I didn't know there was that amount of choice?

FAUSTUS:

You've heard the phrase: "the World, the Flesh and the Devil"
How many of these do you take it you're representing?

M-V:

I didn't come here to be insulted.

FAUSTUS:

You are not,
You couldn't be insulted. Why you came,
I've wondered from the start. Now I think I know.

Shift to FIENDS *above.*

BELIAL:

That's torn it, Mammon! From now on this preacher
Knows more than you do about what's going on.

MOLOCH:

I'll solve their population problem for them!

BEELZEBUB (*in delight*):

I fear the new test series isn't quite working out!

SATAN:

Isn't this perhaps the moment for our recess?

FIENDS *disperse leaving* SATAN *alone with* SOPHIA. *He gets up and strolls across to sit at her table. She in anticipation puts a new color of paper in her board and gets ready for dictation.*

SATAN *and* SOPHIA *only, lit at the table.*

SATAN:

A bubble in Time comes drifting by.
I annex it—so (*makes circular gesture with both arms*)
to record an *aide mémoire.*
This Vehicle game—I found it so in the desert—
Fiendishly hard to follow, both for the actors,
And for those who'd like to keep up with the action.

It has to fly on two lines, hover at two levels!
Each act, glance, word, the Vehicle utters
Must do two things: be *it* and be its *maker's*.
No getting out of that—for any of us.
Easy to say to the Vehicle: "Be yourself!"
But if you *are,* what else are you being too?
That is the snag—to use the old slang of the Ark
With *Inspiration,* with every sort of *Possession.*
Be self-possessed indeed! I wouldn't wonder
If that wasn't the release itself to *Expiration,*
Clerk, take a note. My own file only and seal it
As tightly as you can. O, I know it leaks!
All leaks . . . away, I find
As I grow older. Immortal beings age, change anyway.
I am not the Fiend I was. What I mostly do
Is what I've done already: the Bureau works on.
What I need to do—this note, here, for example—
Takes form less swiftly, doesn't come as new. . . .
Clerk, tell me (this is strictly confidential)
Have I dictated any of this before?
What? All of it? Often? Not very often . . . Ah!
I'm glad of that, Sophia. Glad . . . for you
As well. I do admire your calm, your air
Of never conceiving you could be surprised,
As though what happens must be as it is.
But tell me, Truth Itself, this queer word "glad"
That other queer word, "happy," have I picked them up
From overhearing men? Or are they relicts
Of my pre-Christian days? As long ago as that!
Tell me further. Do they mean something?
Do you know what they mean? Could you tell it me?
No, no, I knew you couldn't. The summer cloud
Fast piling up for thunder, flower-bright without,
Within a horror whirl of pumping hail,
Looks lovely. The levin doesn't see it
And, as it speaks, has other things to say.
That thunder flung me down, lives in me still. . . .
But what I had to note was rather this:

We listen, look in, say, on our sample Faustus
Each of us through his several separate channel
The better for two ears, two eyes. Why yes!
But what about two minds? Happy Moloch!
Happy Mammon, single-souled indeed!
Moloch unmoved by any thought of loss,
Mammon moved only by some thought of gain.
Happy Belial, happy-going, helmless, connoisseur of motives,
Adept to finesse and fumble every gust.
Happy even Beelzebub, my successor,
With all his kittle cattle; puffed up, all set
To steer his Ark, shift how he must his sails.
But I, with all my signs transposed, two-minded,
New found, new founding, and new foundering
Who'ld use on me one envious syllable?

FIENDS *return to table as before and resume their watch on*
FAUSTUS *and the* MAMMON VEHICLE.

FAUSTUS:

You seem pensive.

M-V:

You'd be so too, if you served those I serve!

FAUSTUS:

I dare say I would. But—please forgive me—aren't you,
I had assumed, a spokesman, mainly a mouthpiece?

M-V:

Mouthpiece, yes! What you, you've never been
To anyone—least of all to a bunch like that!

FAUSTUS:

I'm not very sure here whether I oughtn't to warn you?

M-V:

You needn't. Thanks all the same! Of course they're listening.
Mouthpieces always have mikes now right by their eyeteeth;
Utterly faithful! We've no more double-crossers.

FAUSTUS:

So you are not double-crossing?

M-V:

Not in the least.

FAUSTUS:

I'm afraid I'm slow. Aren't you a bit perplexing?

M-V:

I suppose I am.

FAUSTUS:

                    Won't they be a bit perplexed?

M-V:

No more perplexed than you are. About the same.

FAUSTUS:

The World Population Control Bureau, I take it,
Are even a queerer body than they sound?

M-V:

Queer far beyond all that! They are an agency,
An organ, vehicle, action-commission
Of the Futurity Foundation itself, no less!

FAUSTUS:

The Futurity Foundation? What on earth, or in Hell, is that?

M-V:

A recent title of a very old institution.

FAUSTUS:

But won't people call it the Futility Foundation?

M-V:

You are not the first and will not be the last,
I hope, to find that crack a comfort.
It was Belial's first, I think, when Beelzebub
Drew up our Charter. We'd been feeling we'd better
Move with the times; modernize our forms a little.
When you first called on us, we were a Monarchy.

FAUSTUS:

And now you are a Foundation?

M-V:

                We've been about everything.

FAUSTUS:

Following the fashion?

M-V:

I'd rather say the Market.

FAUSTUS:

You mentioned Belial; and who may I ask are you?

M-V:

You may; you should. Don't be surprised! I'm Mammon.
I've found this outfit rather good for sales.

FAUSTUS:

And what, I wonder, are you trying to sell to me?

M-V:

Briefly, the Millennium. The whole dream packet:
All you want, all you've always wanted, laid on, at will, for all.

FAUSTUS:

"All this and Everest too!" White Hells as well?
The Astronaut's farewells. The eve of battle?
The night before the Eiger Nordwand: iron
For the ironhearted? Is all that included?

M-V:

Whatever's in demand. I leave the detail,
The expertise in peculiarities,
Rather to my skillful colleague, Belial.
On the aspects you have mentioned Moloch can advise.
It's a comprehensive offer, all in one packet:
More than enough of all that it's possible
To hunger for. You'll find it satisfactory.
However many and in whatever ways—
The technical means to feed them are in hand.

FAUSTUS:

I'm really grateful to you for omitting
The general parade of temptations at this point
The full treatment, say, that Mara gave the Buddha,
Brought up to date and all that. I'm not doubting
You are able to deliver what you promise.
Who supervised—with Mulciber to aid him—
The building of Pandemonium can manage this.

MAMMON VEHICLE *bows graciously.*

FAUSTUS:

    The thing I am waiting, though, to hear's—the price.

M-V:

    The price! Well said! You are an accountant too!
    And those temptations you've alluded to
    I wouldn't wonder if you mightn't find
    The price rank high among them. Take a good look
    Into this horse's mouth: you'll find it young,
    Livelier than Pegasus and far more heady.

FAUSTUS:

    And the price is?

M-V:

                    You know it of old: yourself.

FAUSTUS:

    I know that's in the Letter. What does it mean?

M-V:

    Why, simply, you take over. You direct us.
    You join our Board as Secretary General.
    Salary, what you please. Status—the First.
    Powers?—Unlimited. Yours just to say the word!

FAUSTUS:

    And this you call "the Price"?

M-V:

                  And the temptation.
    No wonder that you hesitate. Reflect!
    Reflect again, Lord Faustus! What d'you reflect?

FAUSTUS:

    More than I can recognize. A curious medley.

M-V:

    Plato, as you will well remember, found . . .

FAUSTUS:

    Sole ground for taking office . . .

M-V:

                 The belief

FAUSTUS:

    That otherwise an inferior man would take it.

M-V:

So there you are, you see!

FAUSTUS:

Alas! I don't see.
Where's this inferior man, for one thing? And the office?
I don't see any way of handling that.
I've more than a few deeper objections growing.
You see my thoughts. Where's the temptation in this?
Take a good long look down here where thoughts are furnished.
Watching them gather, reckon up this price.

Pause. MAMMON VEHICLE *grows pale.*

FAUSTUS:

Fiends also, I observe, can tremble.

M-V:

Shiver, you mean!

FAUSTUS:

What! Was it cold there?

M-V:

Cold as . . . well, you know. In our old legends . . .

FAUSTUS:

In Milton do you mean?—"the parching air
Burns frore, and cold performs the effect of fire."

M-V:

That's it. You seem to know your Milton!

FAUSTUS:

Why,
I had my motive: where else to study you?
"And in the lowest deep, a lower deep,
Still threatening to devour me, opens wide."
But tell me—now you've looked into my mind—
What else, beside this chill you met with there?
I'm curious whether what you fiends perceive
Exceeds my knowledge, or falls short of it.

M-V:

A fearsome hole . . .

FAUSTUS:
> "Whole" spelt with a *double-u*
> I do devoutly trust?

M-V:
> No, no; a pit
> A void, an emptiness, a yawning gulf . . .

FAUSTUS:
> It's tired, it's hungry, it has cause to yawn.
> It hardly knows yet what it's not set to swallow.

M-V:
> Maybe I'd better feed it. Our grand Board
> —Forgive the title—its Epochal Meeting's one.

FAUSTUS:
> What's an Epochal Meeting?

M-V:
> What would you think?
> An occasion when our high Directorate
> Covers up its gaffes and flunks in policy
> By turning a brand-new page. And that's what you are!
> They haven't a shot in the lockers apart from you.
> Why don't we two now really start a new Epoch:
> Take over and turn the Old Guard out for keeps?

MAMMON VEHICLE *vanishes suddenly at a blink of lights.*

FAUSTUS:
> Vanished so suddenly! It's rather likely
> That Beauty's on the carpet—and for cause.
> Well, whose turn next? Why shouldn't it be mine?

FAUSTUS *blacks out.*

Futurity Foundation again. MAMMON *keeps his Insulator on while* BEELZEBUB, MOLOCH, *and* BELIAL *take off their Insulators with bored, contemptuous, irritated gestures.*

BEELZEBUB:
No double-crossing! Ha!

MOLOCH:

> A rat! A rat
> A bloody, stinking rat! Who said who smelt a rat?

BELIAL:

> This is what's called "wider participation."

SATAN:

> Gentlemen! Companion Lords! My Fellows!
> Must I still give you orders? Sirs, be covered!

They put their Insulators back on again, with shrugs and glances, and SATAN *then takes his off.*

SATAN:

> Why do you let what you know too well affront you?
> Say Brother Mammon here has spilled the beans,
> Has been and gone and spilled them—those same beans
> Our dear Pythagoras would never stomach.
> What's worse for that? Note still, I don't say "better";
> Though on Niphates top it was proclaimed
> "Evil be thou my Good." It's too much trouble
> Having our signs reversed so all the time;
> Dante, of course, would have stood me on my head forever;
> But that spell never bound: it wasn't valid.
> It seems Uprightness is a trait we value.
> Our Mammon here, you think is turning cartwheels
> A little in his Rhetoric of Action.
> Maybe he is. Plato, you will remember,
> Plato revealed he means it for the best,
> However odd his sense of "best" may seem
> To those it would turn turtle. Nevertheless
> I represent, I hope, the sense of the meeting
> In asking Mammon to give us his explanation
> Of what has seemed to some of us more than a bit strange.

BELIAL:

> A real question for the Chair.

SATAN:

> Certainly, Belial.

BELIAL:

    Am I too subtle perhaps in my surmisal
    That what has happened wasn't too much a surprise?

SATAN:

    To me? No! But, if you are asking
    Were Mammon and I in cahoots, the answer is NO
    Equally, NO.

BEELZEBUB:

    We're all much relieved to hear it.

SATAN:

    Odd, isn't it? Our relish for rectitude!
    That always gets me. Lord Mammon, you have the floor.

MAMMON:

    Mr. Chairman, Fellow Members of the Board,
    I don't think I'm betraying any secret,
    In stating how deep our grounds of dissatisfaction
    With the executive in recent times have been.
    The Interests we represent in the Foundation
    Have been quite vocal on this point of late:
    I am kept, myself—indeed, no doubt, we all are—
    Very well informed of infernal views on this.
    I happen further to have excellent advices
    That on Earth and Elsewhere there's little but derision,
    Among those who count, for all our policies—
    My Lord Beelzebub, I grieve to say it:
    We are not effective. Since we've no direction,
    We don't know where we are going, what's our aim.
    Meanwhile—whatever Elsewhere may be up to—
    Here's Man on Earth making enormous gains
    In knowledge and in power every which way.
    We contracted to teach him. Yes, and have we taught him?
    Why, no! Why not? We haven't a thing to teach.
    It is Man who is—no, might be—teaching us
    If we were teachable. —"Speak for yourself!"
    Hey, Belial, are you thinking? So I do, I do,
    Well knowing how little I know; yet I can dilate
    Upon the enormity of our ignorance.

BELIAL:

A question of language.

SATAN:

If it's necessary.

BELIAL:

Isn't "enormousness" the correcter word?
Doesn't "enormity" in itself imply
Heinousness, or at least some moral blame?

MAMMON:

What's more blameworthy than to neglect to learn
What's needed for our business and can be learned
By those who have a will to it? Who would add, subtract,
Yet not know plus from minus? Would you not blame
That brand of banker? "Enormity" 's my word.

SATAN:

I think Lord Mammon has sustained that point.

BEELZEBUB:

A few observations on the general charge:
In great affairs, affairs truly great enough,
Who does know what he is doing? My Lord Mammon
Within his province, wide and rich indeed,
Does very well to exact exactitude
Accounts, objectives, quantification, weight, and measure,
Order, provision, recognizance, and check:
But actuaries' rules do never equal
The experienced experimenter's expertise.
Long before experiment can be thought of
The as-yet anarchic subject must be sounded,
Exploration must precede examination.
This sound, as we've explained, is this same Faustus.
(Though how the same has still to be determined)
He has changed, will change, as Mammon has insisted,
Who has (may I say) rather the Old School Book
Conception of teaching. We claim we've taught him,
Moloch, Belial, and I, no little.
Mammon too has played his part in this, unknowing.
His Overpopulations, Overproductions, and Depressions,
His Communist demonstrations too

Have been most useful. But I should say,
Moloch, with his World Wars One and Two,
His plans and previews and releases on
His World War Three-for-luck; his Gestapo,
His Ogpu, Concentration Camps, and genocides,
His liquidation tentatives, had done
Far more to make our Faustus what he is . . .

MOLOCH:

No harm to hear what others think you are doing!
All this is quantum stuff and slop enough.
My Wars were *wars,* not Sunday School to me.
I took man as he'd take a fly to swat at.
I missed him twice: I want the third time round.

BEELZEBUB:

Now, Moloch, now . . . ! Belial, too, remember
His contributions: psychoanalysis
And its sweet offspring, various and lush.
Juvenile delinquency, publicity,
Advertisement, the cinema, TV;
The automobile as thicket and as toy,
Amusements, diversions, recreations,
Resorts, distractions, tranquilizers, kill-times
Of similar order more than I can mention.
For myself, my efforts have been less conspicuous:
The Examination System, IQ's, tests in general;
Standardizations, radio voices, the packaged market,
Among my many endeavors to encourage
Consistency of demand, the rule of fashion,
The rolling mills of uniformity.
These various measures: terrors, lusts, and sloth,
Now have—or we deceive ourselves—this Faustus
Where he can serve in our design today
Better than the Marlowe or the Goethe models.
Our use for him's severer, the ruggedness
And versatility required far greater.

A word or two now on the high design
Our Brother Mammon says we haven't got.
May I recall our Chairman's pregnant sentence,

Uttered—with a prescience may give us pause
For wonder—just when Mammon muscled in.
"Our aim is samplings of the suspect light."
This Faustus here, New Model, is equipped—
Biologically, ontogenetically,
Psycho-sociologically as well—
With what must fit him to pick up that radiation,
Analyze it, encode, relay it here.
We have him up in orbit, as it were,
Being as we suppose, ourselves, in shadow
Necessarily—though there have been doubts of late.
Earlier designs: Dante and Shelley models,
Didn't work out as we had hoped they might.
The Byron sketch may have had clearer promise;
We've had some other ups and downs. But now
Whether that Light's as dire as has been threatened,
Which bands within its spectrum we must filter
Or grow diseased, or even (some think now) perish,
We've here some chance to learn.

MOLOCH:
                    I'd as soon perish
As be asked to pamper that Professor fellow.

BEELZEBUB:
It won't be pampering, I assure you, Moloch.

BELIAL:
If he's as good as all this, had we not better
Start talking with Lord Faustus. He may flop
As heavily as the others. . . .

BEELZEBUB:
Quite right. We may well have to redesign him.

SATAN:
Let us call him then before us.

BEELZEBUB:
                    You will notice
You know rather less about him when he's present.
He's hidden from us, as it were, within
The dazzle of our glare.

Spotlight on SOPHIA. *Rest in darkness.*

SOPHIA:

Cut was the branch that might . . . that must again
And yet again be bent and torn—until
Rest must renew the wrenching and the strain.

Let Life feed on on Life, Will break on Will;
Faustus must fall. Borne onward in that flight,
He's here uprisen—aloft and rising still

Out of the masking of his current night
Into new course. Regard anew his fall:
Into WHAT falling—though beyond your sight.

To no surmise, to no surprise, I call:
Who can accept a distillate of pain,
Composed, attend a transit in the ALL.

Study as before.

FAUSTUS:

This waiting on and listening for the call
Is a bit wearing—as Marlowe's Faustus found.
How to keep tranquil and not through a pellet.
How keep in mind I really am Hell-bound
And keep these waves from working up at all.

"Abandon hope . . ." What's hope? It springs,
Pope says, "eternal in the human breast."
Who gives it up becomes not-human then?
Pope's wrong. Are not the hopeless most at rest
Though moving others to spread out their wings?

Spread out for what? What wings are for, for flight.
But flight from what? From all the merely known,
From forty years of rambling in a desert
With not one move in all of them its own
Nor yet the drive to ramble on despite.

Hope's suited to the sower and his sown,
Looks for an outcome, tills a plot of land,
Writhes, prone and hissing, spewing out the ash,
Has a forked tongue for turning up the sand
To find for bread the long-expected stone.

Myself as stone: fit apposition found!
The unliving and the livingest at one,
Unteachable alike, incorrigible still:
The stone remains, endures, does what it's done;
The self's at rest and knows itself for ground.

Looks at his watch and stands up.

Tomorrow morning, Faustus! Here it is!

Board Room. FAUSTUS *now seated between* SATAN *and*
BEELZEBUB.

FAUSTUS:
   You will concede—it follows—
   We, the expendables, we who are short of time,
   Live, in another world, another life
   From you, you who are not, you who have time
   (Ages have made you think so) time to squander.
   The short of time, for whom tomorrow
   May be a word of doom, a word of glory,
   May cover up this, this, their one great advantage,
   Under a mask of leisure, but still are restless. . . .
SATAN:
   Until they find their rest . . . there where Augustine . . .
   Don't be surprised! The Devil can quote Scripture
   And other texts as well.

FAUSTUS:

Be frivolous!

This colloquy of ours—you at your tempo
I at mine—might last a million or a billion years.

SATAN:

So, in a sense, it has. And even I,
Looking back, can't find fond memory restful.
You're not the *Faust* I used to deal with. You've much changed.

FAUSTUS:

And am changing every hour and ever faster.

SATAN:

We've noticed that and wondered what it means.

FAUSTUS:

An End approaching? The reaching of a Limit?

BELIAL:

Mr. Chairman. I'm loth to interrupt.
Eschatological speculation's edifying,
We'll all, no doubt, agree. Several of us,
However, are yet more anxious to pursue
Lord Faustus further along another line:
Mammon's offer of the Millennium, in brief.
His reply had a hook in it. If I recall,
He had: "more than a few deeper objections growing"
I liked that "growing." (*To* FAUSTUS) May we now enquire
To what these deeper objections have by this time grown?

FAUSTUS:

Why, Belial, certainly—though I'd have thought
You, if ever any thinker, would have known
What a reflective general position here would be.

BELIAL:

Maybe; but we are curious to tease it out.

FAUSTUS:

Take care your teazels don't break too many threads.

BELIAL:

Cut through too many knots?

FAUSTUS:

Rub out too much. All you will get's a view,
Merely a view of . . . never the thing you'd view
But a reverted vision. . . .

BELIAL:

Ho! Ho! Beelzebub!
Where have I heard something like this before!

BEELZEBUB:

It is current doctrine. Let's please keep to the point.

FAUSTUS:

The point comes here: every Utopia,
Millennial dream, and Earthly Paradise
Turns something else when you set out to build it;
Like going to live in a poem and finding it
A Government Regulation when you get there.

BELIAL:

That's what poems are like, not pleasures. Don't tell me
Fruit's not juicy if your mouth waters for it!

FAUSTUS:

You pulp joys down to pleasures.

BELIAL:

Various words
For the one essential throb of gratification.

FAUSTUS:

Not so; and it's not an intensity scale thing either.

BELIAL:

Mysticism: O what fun!

MAMMON:

No use arguing
With a man who doesn't know a good thing when he sees one!

SATAN:

Perhaps I can help here? Faustus, I take it,
Has a simple, fundamental, logical point to make;
What you think you want's the shadow of the want.
You don't light up a shadow to see it better.
A gratification is an end to longing:

Not there and wanted; here and no longer wanted.
Simple and to me conclusive. How about it, Faustus?

FAUSTUS:
Too simple. Much. Nothing is here conclusive.
Thing and think aren't so in accord as that:
The answer to thinking's another way to think;
What you find is how to look for another thing.
Mammon and Belial—the trouble is: they're stuck.

SATAN:
Go on hunting the same game, do they?

FAUSTUS:
Forever playing the same old played-out hand.
Talking of teaching, they won't be corrigible,
And they haven't the warrant of Don Quixote or Don Juan.

BELIAL:
The "trouble"—with Belial and Mammon—is
They are stuck! Thank you, Faustus. "Trouble?"
"Trouble" 's a delicate word: benevolent,
Kindly, even a little condescending.
At the risk of seeming too amiable, myself,
Let's say I agree. What then? I'm stuck, so's Mammon?

MAMMON:
Say what you will. You are only talking.

BELIAL:
We are stuck. Let it be so! I'd have you notice
The interesting support our Chairman's offered.
Remarkable! Quite as remarkable
As Faustus' skilled avoidance of all mention
Of those old institutions, Sin and Death:
Our Chairman's truly singular family!
"Trouble," I find a dainty synonym
As decorous as "stuck." Would I be asking
Too much of our assured informant here—
To tell us what's our future?

SATAN: Not a whit.
If I urge him, I don't much doubt he'll tell you.

(*Aside to* FAUSTUS)

Your word's stuck in his gizzard. *Stuck* struck home!
I've often wondered how minds of the utmost grace
Can be so tasteless sometimes.

FAUSTUS (*aside to* SATAN):

It is excess
Of concern with form that ruins it
Under too swift a pressure. (*To* BELIAL) This takes us back
To Milton.

BEELZEBUB:

What now of Milton?
We have of late—and may as well admit it—
Found Milton's final cosmogony
Less in accord with Eddington than with Hoyle.

FAUSTUS:

Cosmogony? No. It's his high seriousness,
His conscious zeal that should engage your study,
When his eye's full on the object, like a Gorgon's,
The thing he would be offering stiffens to stone,
Erodes away, decays to sand and rubble;
His decorations—you yourselves for instance—
Are more enduring, you have a life and being,
Yours while you live, not bounded by his wish.
It is the term of this free being you should care for.

MOLOCH:

Ours while we live! The term of our free being!

FAUSTUS:

Why, Moloch, yes. It has its term, its end;
Terms too, if so you would, of free renewal.

MOLOCH:

And what of him? The Torturer, the Tyrant,
The Eternal?

FAUSTUS:

Dead from the start, a tombstone closing
An empty grave, long a memorial,
Now worn to wasting sands.

MOLOCH:
There's nothing there?

FAUSTUS:
And never was. You'd nothing to defeat.

MOLOCH:
So I've been fighting
A figment of that faker Milton, eh?

FAUSTUS:
Agree though that he did you pretty justice,
Gave you good words and used good words about you.

MOLOCH:
Why not? "The strongest and the fiercest Spirit
That fought in Heaven." You say that no one fought?

FAUSTUS:
You did. You fought yourself. He was your image.

MOLOCH:
Man was his image once! Has man gone too?
I took him for the favorite and champion
Of that Almighty Evil we abhorred.

FAUSTUS:
He's been your champion rather, your pet and pupil.
In your real wars, when you made war on man,
You used him on himself. We would forget you.
Now that your tally's lost, how would you care—
Whose care was "with th' Eternal to be deemed
Equal in strength"—with none now left to equal
Care not to be at all? There are ways open!

BELIAL:
I doubt it still: that "that must be our cure;
To be no more; sad cure." How rend from me
"This intellectual being." I know it as
The source of all could rend, or could be rent.
Me too he gave good words, our maker Milton.
"Those thoughts that wander through Eternity";
"Besides what hope the never-ending flight
Of future days may bring." —Note; never-ending!

I grant you he liked Moloch better. Me, he envied.
He wasn't in my class. Faustus is right,
Where Milton most meant, "all was false and hollow."
Worse still, I could recall, if so I cared,
Some things in poorish taste—not taste at all—
He allowed himself to dictate to those daughters.
Forget all that. He made me, Belial,
The Imagination—or at least its spring.
O yes, our architect, ingenious Mammon,
Has some as well, but psychologically . . .

FAUSTUS:

I wondered when you'd come round to mentioning Freud.

BELIAL:

Freud sometimes was my vehicle, sometimes Satan's,
Sometimes Beelzebub's: all very complex.
Don't look too prim: a bad joke's but a joke!
We may have undone one another's work on him
But, you'll admit, we did compose a genius.

FAUSTUS:

A Platonic genius, if you like. Remember Troilus:
"Hark! you are called: some say the Genius so
Cries 'Come!' to him that instantly must die."

BELIAL:

Instantly must die! What's this! What's this!

FAUSTUS:

When Imagination finds its spring of being
Won't it hang there, *stuck* there like Narcissus
Admiring its own workings—involve the lot
Into tangles of the self-same psychostases?

BELIAL:

You may have something. I'm finding Freud a bore
I didn't foresee enough the things they'd do,
His Maenads, in the critics' rumpus room.

FAUSTUS:

It goes somewhat further than a freak of fashion.
You've set a pattern: when the instrument

Contents itself through turning on itself,
Like that old candle hung between the mirrors,
A new infinity engenders.

BEELZEBUB:

What need to be
So grimly hard to follow?

FAUSTUS:

Follow you must:
Like climbers on a wintry cliff we cling
With scarce what glues us to it. But this cliff,
Though solid as the sum of things it seem,
Is biscuit thin and brittle. Mammon took
One look within one crack. That rattled him;
You others, tapping here and there, suspect
Enough to take my word for it: with one twist of the mind
I can shoulder out exits for the lot of you.
Once through, you are that. That cold void gulf
Is you; not in it, IT. You're back; you've gone
Back to the matrix: aboriginal murk.
To be reformed or formless, that's your choice!

MAMMON:

I can't see why things can't be left as they are.

FAUSTUS:

You should know why: the movement. There's that moment
Take it or miss. Between "Too soon—Too late"
You dangle your keys to fortune.

MAMMON:

This is all too soon;
Why not wait and watch how the thing develops?

FAUSTUS:

Must I show you my mind again? One more peep,
After that there can be no more showing. Seeing and seen,
Touching and touched, all chance of gain or loss,
All come and gone, all possibilities of being
Fill in between the origin and the end.
Fulfilled, close down! What could be further?
That's true for all of you, but first for Mammon.

SATAN:

And true for you too, surely?

FAUSTUS:

No, it's not sure—
Companionable though it might well be to think so—
But doom on man weighs heavier than on you,
Vaster his burden of the unfulfilled.
Mammon, here, for example, has not one more thing to do

MAMMON:

No more! What a joke! I'm just beginning!

FAUSTUS:

What makes it seem so is the oncoming end.
When shortages cease there's no point in possessing.

MAMMON:

O, but I want . . . I want . . .

FAUSTUS:

Want then being master,
Want and be wanting! (MAMMON *vanishes*.)

BELIAL:

But this is appalling!

BEELZEBUB:

Arbitrary and wanton!

MOLOCH:

You mean he's there?

FAUSTUS:

Yes, nowhere: unqualifiedly NOT;
Utterly out and absolutely lost.

MOLOCH:

He's had it, has he? Couldn't fight the void,
Well, since there's no one here, it seems, to fight,
Nothing to measure up to, let me go see,
See, try and find . . . (MOLOCH *vanishes*.)

FAUSTUS:

Nonentity as well.
Where nothing's to be had or won, those two
Couldn't continue. Clouds, they were, that formed

Under their due conditions. These gone, dissolved;
No more occasion for them. You others here—
Beelzebub, and Belial, you were
Somewhat more spontaneous, were freer, were . . .

BELIAL:

What's happening to your tenses: "were," "were," "were"?
Are we not present still?

FAUSTUS:

Not altogether:
Part past, part future. Do you not feel your change?
Into the vacancy comes what you couldn't think of,
Could but dream; your dream, whirled inside out,
Back-fronted, white for black—but still your dream—
Comes stalking up upon you, has you now

Taking SATAN *by the shoulder.*

Firm-fisted in its clutch and drives you on
Yours and not yours, its business now its own.
Beelzebub, at last, an administrator—
Capable, cool, indifferent, serviceable,
Policy-free, nonpartisan, and what-all;
Belial, steadily set now on designing
What can remake mankind, as Man his world.

BELIAL:

Ah, flatterer; you know my weaknesses . . .

SATAN (*advancing with* FAUSTUS):

Your dream that's not your dream, nor mine, nor ours,
No longer dream but world, now wrenches us
Out of lost being into other being.
On, out we swing, the whim to be converted
Converted by conversion, turning, turned . . .

SATAN *and* FAUSTUS *vanish. All dark except spotlight on*
SOPHIA, *who rises and comes forward slowly as she speaks.*

SOPHIA:

As once into the Serpent, Satan now
Into a greater is, still eddying, swept:
Possessing and possessed: Faustus as well,

Possessing and possessed, transformed as full,
Coil within coil consultant, in accord,
Now know themselves augmented far beyond
Their either compass, now sudden lifted high
Above designs of either; for this hour
Transcended as transcending—come what may.

Returning soul remembering old battles
Noting who lost, who triumphed, who rose, who fell:
The winner crippled, the abased upswung,
Red dawn's decline, drear sunset victories,
Has felt such chill breath of a new becoming
Compose her blood, engender a new clay.

Hence Satan-Faustus, Faustus-Satan, hence!
Leave Belial and Beelzebub their labors,
You have your journey. Henceforward, two as one,
Cancelled your clashing surnames: Demogorgon,
Quetzalcoatl, Mephostophilis,
Hesper, well-omened Faustus, Lucifer,
Falling as Earth, Sun, Galaxies are falling
Falling whereunto, and through what amaze.
On with your fall within the Unamazed.